A COLLECTION
OF HOPE

HELEN STEINER RICE

BARBOUR
PUBLISHING

A HELEN STEINER RICE ® Product

ISBN 978-1-61626-676-9

eBook Editions:
Adobe Digital Edition (.epub) 978-1-60742-764-3
Kindle and MobiPocket Edition (.prc) 978-1-60742-765-0

Published by Barbour Publishing, Inc., P.O. Box 719, Uhrichsville, Ohio 44683, www.barbourbooks.com

Our mission is to publish and distribute inspirational products offering exceptional value and biblical encouragement to the masses.

 Member of the
Evangelical Christian
Publishers Association

Printed in the United States of America.

CONTENTS

PEACEFUL

REFLECTIONS

*Know that
We love you &
lift up your
name in
our daily
prayers—*

After Each Storm of Life, There's a Rainbow Hope

❧❧❧

The rainbow is God's promise
of hope for you and me,
And though the clouds hang
heavy and the sun we cannot see,
We know above the dark
clouds that fill the stormy sky,
Hope's rainbow will come shining through
when the clouds have drifted by.

Jackie Casson

A Beautiful Beginning for Peace on Earth

Let us all remember when
our faith is running low,
Christ is more than just a figure
wrapped in an ethereal glow. . .
For He came and dwelled among
us and He knows our every need,
And He loves and understands
us and forgives each sinful deed.
He was crucified and buried
and rose again in glory,
And His promise of salvation
makes the wondrous Christmas story
An abiding reassurance that
the little Christ child's birth
Was the beautiful beginning of
God's plan for peace on earth.

No Favor Do I Seek Today

❧◦❧

I come not to ask, to plead, or implore —
I just come to tell You how much I adore You.
For to kneel in Your presence makes me feel blessed,
For I know that You know all my needs best,
And it fills me with joy just to linger with you,
As my soul You replenish and my heart You renew.
For prayer is much more than just asking for things —
It's the peace and contentment that quietness brings.
So thank You again for Your mercy and love
And for making me heir to Your kingdom above.

It's a Wonderful World

In spite of the fact we complain and lament
And view this old world with much discontent,
Deploring conditions and grumbling because
There's so much injustice and so many flaws,
It's a wonderful world and it always will be
If we keep our eyes open and focused to see
The wonderful things we are capable of
When we open our hearts to God and His love.

THE HAPPINESS YOU ALREADY HAVE

Memories are treasures that
time cannot destroy,
They are the happy pathway
to yesterday's bright joy.

The Peace of Meditation

So we may know God better
and feel His quiet power,
Let us daily keep in silence a meditation hour.
For to understand God's greatness
and to use His gifts each day,
The soul must learn to meet
Him in a meditative way.
For nature's great forces
are found in quiet things
Like softly falling snowflakes
drifting down on angels' wings
So let us plan with prayerful
care to always allocate
A certain portion of each day
to be still and meditate.
For when everything is quiet
and we're lost in meditation,
Our souls are then preparing
for a deeper dedication
That will make it wholly
possible to quietly endure
The violent world around us,
for in God we are secure.

LIFE

A little laughter, a little song,
A little teardrop
When things go wrong,
A little calm
And a little strife
A little loving
And that is life.

What More Can You Ask?

God's love endures forever—
what a wonderful thing to know
When the tides of life run against you
and your spirit is downcast and low.
God's kindness is ever around you
always ready to freely impart
Strength to your faltering spirit,
cheer to your lonely heart.
God's presence is ever beside you,
as near as the reach of your hand.
You have but to tell Him your troubles—
there is nothing He won't understand. . .
And knowing God's love is unfailing,
and His mercy unending and great,
You have but to trust in His promise,
"God comes not too soon or too late."
So wait with a heart that is patient
for the goodness of God to prevail,
For never do prayers go unanswered,
and His mercy and love never fail.

Peace Begins in the Home and the Heart

Peace is not something you fight
for with bombs and missiles that kill.
Peace is attained in the silence that
comes when the heart stands still.
For hearts that are restless and
warlike with longings that never cease
Can never contribute ideas that
bring the world nearer to peace.
For as dew never falls on a morning
that follows a dark, stormy night,
The peace and grace of our Father
fall not on a soul in flight.
So if we seek peace for all people,
there is but one place to begin,
And the armament race will not win it,
for the fortress of peace is within.

THE MASTERPIECE

Framed by the vast, unlimited sky,
Bordered by mighty waters,
Sheltered by beautiful woodland groves,
Scented with flowers that bloom and die,
Protected by giant mountain peaks—
The land of the great unknown—
Snowcapped and towering, a nameless place
That beckons man on as the gold he seeks,
Bubbling with life and earthly joys,
Reeking with pain and mortal strife,
Dotted with wealth and material gains,
Built on ideals of girls and boys,
Streaked with toil, opportunity's banner unfurled
Stands out the masterpiece of art
Painted by the one great God,
A picture of the world.

LEARN TO REST

We all need short vacations
in life's fast and maddening race
An interlude of quietness from
the constant jet-age pace,
So when your day is pressure-packed
and your hours are all too few,
Just close your eyes and meditate
and let God talk to you.
For when we keep on pushing,
we're not following in God's way
We are foolish, selfish robots
mechanized to fill each day
With unimportant trivia that
makes life more complex
And gives us greater problems to irritate and vex.
So when your nervous network
becomes a tangled mess,
Just close your eyes in silent prayer
and ask the Lord to bless
Each thought that you are thinking,
each decision you must make,
As well as every word you speak
and every step you take
For only by the grace of God
can you gain self-control,
And only meditative thoughts
can restore your peace and soul.

The Comfort and Sweetness of Peace

After the clouds, the sunshine,
After the winter, the spring,
After the shower, the rainbow—
For life is a changeable thing.
After the night, the morning,
Bidding all darkness cease,
After life's cares and sorrows,
The comfort and sweetness of peace.

$\mathcal{A}$ Word of Understanding

May peace and understanding
Give you strength and courage, too,
And may the hours and days ahead
Hold a new hope for you;
For the sorrow that is yours today
Will pass away; and then
You'll find the sun of happiness
Will shine for you again.

THE COMFORT

OF FRIENDS

DISCOURAGEMENT AND DREAMS

So many things in the line of duty
Drain us of effort and leave us no beauty,
And the dust of the soul grows thick and unswept,
The spirit is drenched in tears unwept.
But just as we fall beside the road,
Discouraged with life and
bowed down with our load,
We lift our eyes, and what seemed a dead end
Is the street of dreams where we meet a friend.

Friends Are Life's Gift of Love

If people like me didn't know people like you,
Life would lose its meaning and its richness, too.
For the friends that we make are life's gift of love,
And I think friends are sent right from heaven above.
And thinking of you somehow makes me feel
That God is love and He's very real.

The Golden Chain of Friendship

Friendship is a golden chain,
the links are friends so dear,
And like a rare and precious jewel,
it's treasured more each year.
It's clasped together firmly
with a love that's deep and true,
And it's rich with happy memories
and fond recollections, too.
Time can't destroy its beauty,
for as long as memory lives,
Years can't erase the pleasure
that the joy of friendship gives.
For friendship is a priceless gift
that can't be bought or sold,
And to have an understanding friend
is worth far more than gold.
And the golden chain of friendship
is a strong and blessed tie
Binding kindred hearts together
as the years go passing by.

THE GIFT OF FRIENDSHIP

Friendship is a priceless gift
that cannot be bought or sold,
But its value is far greater than
a mountain made of gold—
For gold is cold and lifeless,
it can neither see nor hear,
And in the time of trouble it
is powerless to cheer.
It has no ears to listen,
no heart to understand,
It cannot bring you comfort or
reach out a helping hand—
So when you ask God for a gift
be thankful if He sends
Not diamonds, pearls, or riches,
but the love of real true friends.

THE JOY OF UNSELFISH GIVING

Time is not measured by the years that you live
But by the deeds that you do and
the joy that you give.
And from birthday to birthday,
the good Lord above
Bestows on His children the gift of His love,
Asking us only to share it with others
By treating all people not as strangers
but brothers.
And each day as it comes brings
a chance to each one
To live to the fullest, leaving nothing undone
That would brighten the life or lighten the load
Of some weary traveler lost on life's road.
So it doesn't matter how long we may live
If as long as we live we unselfishly give.

A Friend Is a Gift from God

Among the great and glorious
gifts our heavenly Father sends
Is the gift of understanding
that we find in loving friends.
For in this world of trouble
that is filled with anxious care,
Everybody needs a friend in
whom they're free to share
The little secret heartaches
that lay heavy on the mind—
Not just a mere acquaintance
but someone who's just our kind.
For somehow in the generous
heart of loving, faithful friends,
The good God, in His charity
and wisdom, always sends
A sense of understanding
and the power of perception
And mixes these fine qualities
with kindness and affection.
And often just without a word
there seems to be a union
Of thoughts and kindred feelings,
for God gives true friends communion.

Life Is a Garden

Life is a garden; good friends are the flowers,
And times spent together life's happiest hours.
And friendship, like flowers, blooms ever more fair
When carefully tended by dear friends who care.
And life's lovely garden would be sweeter by far
If all who passed through it were as nice as you are.

STRANGERS ARE FRIENDS WE HAVEN'T MET YET

God knows no strangers, He loves us all,
The poor, the rich, the great, the small.
He is a friend who is always there
To share our troubles and lessen our care.
For no one is a stranger in God's sight,
For God is love, and in His light
May we, too, try in our small way
To make new friends from day to day.
So pass no stranger with an unseeing eye,
For God may be sending a new friend by.

Unexpected Angels

The unexpected kindness
from an unexpected place,
A hand outstretched in friendship,
a smile on someone's face,
A word of understanding
spoken in a time of trial
Are unexpected miracles that
make life more worthwhile.
We know not how it happened
that in an hour of need
Somebody out of nowhere
proved to be a friend indeed. . .
For God has many messengers
we fail to recognize,
But He sends them when we need them,
and His ways are wondrous and wise. . .
So keep looking for an angel and
keep listening to hear,
For on life's busy, crowded streets,
you will find God's presence near.

The Garden of Friendship

There is no garden
So complete
But roses could make
The place more sweet.
There is no life
So rich and rare
But one more friend
Could enter there.
Like roses in a garden
Kindness fills the air
With a certain bit of sweetness
As it touches everywhere.

My God Is No Stranger

God is no stranger in a faraway place
He's as close as the wind that blows 'cross my face.
It's true I can't see the wind as it blows,
But I feel it around me and my heart surely knows
That God's mighty hand can be felt everywhere,
For there's nothing on earth that is not in God's care.
The sky and the stars, the waves and the sea,
The dew on the grass, the leaves on a tree
Are constant reminders of God and His nearness
Proclaiming His presence with crystal-like clearness.
So how could I think God was far, far away
When I feel Him beside me every hour of the day?
And I've plenty of reasons to know God's my friend,
And this is one friendship that time cannot end.

JOY IN ALL CIRCUMSTANCES

How Great the Yield from a Fertile Field

୧ୠୡ୭ଵ

The farmer plows through the fields of green,
And the blade of the plow is sharp and keen,
But the seed must be sown to bring forth grain,
For nothing is born without suffering and pain,
And God never plows in the soul of man
Without intention and purpose and plan. . .
So whenever you feel the plow's sharp blade
Let not your heart be sorely afraid,
For like the farmer, God chooses a field
From which He expects an excellent yield. . .
So rejoice though your heart be broken in two—
God seeks to bring forth a rich harvest in you.

Meet Life's Trials with Smiles

There are times when life overwhelms
us and our trials seem too many to bear,
It is then we should stop to remember
God is standing by ready to share
The uncertain hours that confront
us and fill us with fear and despair,
For God in His goodness has promised
that the cross that He gives us to wear
Will never exceed our endurance or
be more than our strength can bear. . .
And secure in that blessed assurance,
we can smile as we face tomorrow,
For God holds the key to the future,
and no sorrow or care we need borrow.

Make Your Day Bright
by Thinking Right

Don't start your day by supposin'
that trouble is just ahead,
It's better to stop supposin' and
start with a prayer instead. . .
And make it a prayer of thanksgiving
for the wonderful things God has wrought,
Like the beautiful sunrise and sunset,
God's gifts that are free and not bought. . .
For what is the use of supposin' that
dire things could happen to you,
Worrying about some misfortune that
seldom if ever comes true. . .
But instead of just idle supposin',
step forward to meet each new day
Secure in the knowledge God's near you
to lead you each step of the way. . .
For supposin' the worst things will happen
only helps to make them come true,
And you darken the bright, happy moments
that the dear Lord has given to you. . .
So if you desire to be happy and get
rid of the misery of dread,
Just give up supposin' the worst things
and look for the best things instead.

Expectation! Anticipation! Realization!

God gives us a power we so seldom employ,
For we're so unaware it is filled with such joy.
The gift that God gives us is anticipation,
Which we can fulfill with sincere expectation,
For there's power in belief when
we think we will find
Joy for the heart and peace for the mind,
And believing the day will bring a surprise
Is not only pleasant but surprisingly wise.
For we open the door to let joy walk through
When we learn to expect the best,
and the most, too,
And believing we'll find a happy surprise
Makes reality out of a fancied surmise.

After the Winter God Sends the Spring

Springtime is a season of
hope and joy and cheer—
There's beauty all around us to
see and touch and hear.
So no matter how downhearted
and discouraged we may be,
New hope is born when we behold
leaves budding on a tree
Or when we see a timid flower
push through the frozen sod
And open wide in glad surprise
its petaled eyes to God.
For this is just God saying,
"Lift up your eyes to Me,
And the bleakness of your spirit,
like the budding springtime tree,
Will lose its wintry darkness and
your heavy heart will sing."
For God never sends the winter
without the joy of spring.

Adversity Can Bless Us

The way we use adversity is
strictly our own choice,
For in God's hands, adversity
can make the heart rejoice.
For everything God sends to us,
no matter in what form,
Is sent with plan and purpose;
for by the fierceness of a storm,
The atmosphere is changed and cleared,
and the earth is washed and clean,
And the high winds of adversity
can make restless souls serene.
And while it's very difficult
for mankind to understand
God's intentions and His purpose
and the workings of His hand,
If we observe the miracles that happen every day,
We cannot help but be convinced
that in His wondrous way
God makes what seemed unbearable
and painful and distressing
Easily acceptable when we view it as a blessing.

Giving Is the Key to Living

Every day is a reason for giving
And giving is the key to living.
So let us give ourselves away,
Not just today but every day,
And remember, a kind and thoughtful deed
Or a hand outstretched in a time of need
Is the rarest of gifts, for it is a part,
Not of the purse but a loving heart.
And he who gives of himself will find
True joy of heart and peace of mind.

LOOK ON THE SUNNY SIDE

There are always two sides, the good and the bad,
The dark and the light, the sad and the glad.
But in looking back over the good and the bad,
We're aware of the number of
good things we've had,
And in counting our blessings,
we find when we're through
We've no reason at all to complain or be blue.
So thank God for the good things
He has already done,
And be grateful to Him for the battles you've won
And know that the same God
who helped you before
Is ready and willing to help you once more.
Then with faith in your heart,
reach out for God's hand
And accept what He sends,
though you can't understand.
For our Father in heaven always
knows what is best,
And if you trust His wisdom,
your life will be blessed.
For always remember that whatever betide you,
You are never alone, for God is beside you.

LIVES DISTRESSED
CANNOT BE BLESSED

Refuse to be discouraged, refuse to be distressed,
For when we are despondent,
our lives cannot be blessed,
For doubt and fear and worry close
the door to faith and prayer,
And there's no room for blessings
when we're lost in deep despair.
So remember when you're troubled
with uncertainty and doubt,
It is best to tell our Father what
our fear is all about,
For unless we seek His guidance
when troubled times arise,
We are bound to make decisions
that are twisted and unwise,
But when we view our problems
through the eyes of God above,
Misfortunes turn to blessings and
hatred turns to love.

A Sure Way to a Happy Day

❧

Happiness is something we create in our minds;
It's not something you search for and so seldom find.
It's just waking up and beginning the day
By counting our blessings and kneeling to pray.
It's giving up thoughts that breed discontent
And accepting what comes as a gift heaven-sent.
It's giving up wishing for things we have not
And making the best of whatever we've got.
It's knowing that life is determined for us
And pursuing our tasks without fret, fume, or fuss.
For it's by completing what God gives us to do
That we find real contentment and happiness, too.

Be Glad

Be glad that your life has been full and complete,
Be glad that you've tasted the bitter and sweet.
Be glad that you've walked in sunshine and rain,
Be glad that you've felt both pleasure and pain.
Be glad that you've had such a full, happy life,
Be glad for your joy as well as your strife.
Be glad that you've walked with courage each day,
Be glad you've had strength for each step of the way.
Be glad for the comfort that you've found in prayer.
Be glad for God's blessings, His love, and His care.

ABUNDANT
THANKSGIVING

New Year Meditation

What better time and what better season,
What greater occasion or more wonderful reason
To kneel down in prayer and lift our hands high
To the God of creation, who made earth and sky,
Who sent us His Son to live here among men—
And the message He brought is as
true now as then. . .
So at this glad season, when there's joy everywhere,
Let us meet our Redeemer at the altar of prayer,
Asking Him humbly to bless all of our days
And grant us forgiveness for our erring ways. . .
And though we're unworthy, dear Father above,
Accept us today and let us dwell in Thy love
So we may grow stronger upheld by Thy grace,
And with Thy assistance be ready to face
All the temptations that fill every day,
And hold on to our hands when
we stumble and stray. . .
And thank You, dear God, for the
year that now ends
And for the great blessing of loved
ones and friends.

A Heart Full of Thanksgiving

Everyone needs someone to be thankful for,
And each day of life we are aware of this more,
For the joy of enjoying and the fullness of living
Are found only in hearts that are filled
with thanksgiving.

A Thankful Heart

Take nothing for granted, for whenever you do,
The joy of enjoying is lessened for you.
For we rob our own lives much
more than we know
When we fail to respond or in any way show
Our thanks for the blessings that daily are ours—
The warmth of the sun, the fragrance of flowers,
The beauty of twilight, the freshness of dawn,
The coolness of dew on a green velvet lawn,
The kind little deeds so thoughtfully done,
The favors of friends and the love that someone
Unselfishly gives us in a myriad of ways,
Expecting no payment and no words of praise.
Oh, great is our loss when we no longer find
A thankful response to things of this kind.
For the joy of enjoying and the fullness of living
Are found in the heart that is
filled with thanksgiving.

A PRAYER OF THANKS

Thank You, God, for the
beauty around me everywhere,
The gentle rain and glistening dew,
the sunshine and the air,
The joyous gift of feeling the soul's soft,
whispering voice
That speaks to me from deep within
and makes my heart rejoice.

Showers of Blessings

Each day there are showers of
blessings sent from the Father above,
For God is a great, lavish giver,
and there is no end to His love.
And His grace is more than sufficient,
His mercy is boundless and deep,
And His infinite blessings are countless,
and all this we're given to keep
If we but seek God and find Him
and ask for a bounteous measure
Of this wholly immeasurable offering
from God's inexhaustible treasure.
For no matter how big man's dreams are,
God's blessings are infinitely more,
For always God's giving is greater
than what man is asking for.

Thank You God for Everything

All too often we accept without
any thanks or praise
The gifts God sends as blessings
each day in many ways.
And so at this time we offer up a prayer
To thank You, God, for giving us
a lot more than our share.
First, thank You for the little
things that often come our way—
The things we take for granted
and don't mention when we pray—
The unexpected courtesy, the thoughtful,
kindly deed,
A hand reached out to help us
in the time of sudden need.
Oh make us more aware, dear God,
of little daily graces
That come to us with sweet surprise
from never-dreamed-of places.
Then thank You for the miracles
we are much too blind to see,
And give us new awareness
of our many gifts from Thee.
And help us to remember that
the key to life and living
Is to make each prayer a prayer of thanks
and each day a day of thanksgiving.

IF YOU MEET GOD
IN THE MORNING

Each day at dawning I lift my heart high
And raise up my eyes to the infinite sky.
I watch the night vanish as a new day is born,
And I hear the birds sing on the wings of the morn.
I see the dew glisten in crystal-like splendor
While God, with a touch that is gentle and tender,
Wraps up the night and softly tucks it away
And hangs out the sun to herald a new day.
And so I give thanks and my heart kneels to pray,
"God, keep me and guide me and go with me today."

A THANKSGIVING DAY PRAYER

Faith of our fathers, renew us again
And make us a nation of God-fearing men
Seeking Thy guidance, Thy love, and Thy will,
For we are but pilgrims in search of Thee still. . .
And gathered together on Thanksgiving Day,
May we lift up our hearts and our hands as we pray
To thank You for blessings we so little merit,
And grant us Thy love and teach us to share it.

Things to Be Thankful For

The good, green earth beneath our feet,
The air we breathe, the food we eat,
Some work to do, a goal to win,
A hidden longing deep within
That spurs us on to bigger things
And helps us meet what each day brings—
All these things and many more
Are things we should be thankful for. . .
And most of all, our thankful prayers
Should rise to God because He cares.

So Many Reasons to Love the Lord

Thank You, God, for little
things that come unexpectedly
To brighten up a dreary day
that dawned so dismally.
Thank You, God, for sending
a happy thought my way
To blot out my depression on a disappointing day.
Thank You, God, for brushing
the dark clouds from my mind
And leaving only sunshine
and joy of heart behind.
Oh God, the list is endless of
the things to thank You for,
But I take them all for granted
and unconsciously ignore
That everything I think or do,
each movement that I make,
Each measured, rhythmic heartbeat,
each breath of life I take
Is something You have given me
for which there is no way
For me in all my smallness to in any way repay.

UNFAILING LOVE

*H*E LOVES YOU

It's amazing and incredible,
but it's as true as it can be—
God loves and understands us all,
and that means you and me.
His grace is all-sufficient for
both the young and old,
For the lonely and the timid,
for the brash and for the bold.
His love knows no exceptions,
so never feel excluded,
No matter who or what you are,
your name has been included. . .
And no matter what your past has been,
trust God to understand,
And no matter what your problem is,
just place it in His hand. . .
For in all our unloveliness this
great God loves us still—
He loved us since the world began,
and what's more, He always will!

Stepping Stones to God

An aching heart is but a stepping stone
To greater joy than you've ever known,
For things that cause the heart to ache
Until you think that it must break
Become the strength by which we climb
To higher heights that are sublime
And feel the radiance of God's smiles
When we have soared above life's trials.
So when you're overwhelmed with fears
And all your hopes are drenched in tears,
Think not that life has been unfair
And given you too much to bear,
For God has chosen you because,
With all your weaknesses and flaws,
He feels that you are worthy of
The greatness of his wondrous love.

God's Love Is a Haven in the Storms of Life

~~~~

God's love is like an island in
life's ocean vast and wide,
A peaceful, quiet shelter from
the restless, rising tide.
God's love is like a fortress,
and we seek protection there
When the waves of tribulation
seem to drown us in despair.
God's love is a sanctuary where
our souls can find sweet rest
From the struggle and the tension
of life's fast and futile quest.
God's love is like a tower rising
far above the crowd,
And God's smile is like the sunshine breaking
through the threatening cloud.
God's love is like a beacon burning
bright with faith and prayer,
And through all the changing scenes
of life we can find a haven there.

Never Be Discouraged

There is really nothing we need
know or even try to understand
If we refuse to be discouraged
and trust God's guiding hand,
So take heart and meet each minute
with faith in God's great love,
Aware that every day of life is
controlled by God above
And never dread tomorrow
or what the future brings
Just pray for strength and courage
and trust God in all things,
And never grow discouraged—
be patient and just wait,
For God never comes too early,
and He never comes too late.

THE MAGIC OF LOVE

Love is like magic and it always will be,
For love still remains life's sweet mystery.
Love works in ways that are
wondrous and strange,
And there's nothing in life that
love cannot change.
Love can transform the most commonplace
Into beauty and splendor and
sweetness and grace.
Love is unselfish, understanding, and kind,
For it sees with its heart and not with its mind.
Love gives and forgives; there is nothing too much
For love to heal with its magic touch.
Love is the language that every heart speaks,
For love is the one thing that every heart seeks. . .
And where there is love God, too, will abide
And bless the family residing inside.

Wings of Love

The priceless gift of life is love,
For with the help of God above
Love can change the human race
And make this world a better place. . .
For love dissolves all hate and fear
And makes our vision bright and clear
So we can see and rise above
Our pettiness on wings of love.

Do Not Be Anxious

Do not be anxious, said our Lord,
Have peace from day to day—
The lilies neither toil nor spin,
Yet none are clothed as they.
The meadowlark with sweetest song
Fears not for bread or nest
Because he trusts our Father's love,
And God knows what is best.

God Is Never beyond Our Reach

No one ever sought the Father
and found He was not there,
And no burden is too heavy
to be lightened by a prayer.
No problem is too intricate,
and no sorrow that we face
Is too deep and devastating
to be softened by His grace.
No trials and tribulations are
beyond what we can bear
If we share them with our Father
as we talk to Him in prayer. . .

God Loves Us

We are all God's children
and He loves us, every one.
He freely and completely
forgives all that we have done,
Asking only if we're ready to
follow where He leads,
Content that in His wisdom
He will answer all our needs.

The Hand of God Is Everywhere

It's true we have never looked on His face,
But His likeness shines forth from every place,
For the hand of God is everywhere
Along life's busy thoroughfare,
And His presence can be felt and seen
Right in the midst of our daily routine.
Things we touch and see and feel
Are what make God so very real.

SEASONS OF HOPE

The Blessings of God's Seasons

We know we must pass through
the seasons God sends,
Content in the knowledge that everything ends,
And oh, what a blessing to know there are reasons
And to find that our souls must,
too, have their seasons—
Bounteous seasons and barren ones, too,
Times for rejoicing and times to be blue—
But meeting these seasons of dark desolation
With the strength that is born of anticipation
Comes from knowing that every season of sadness
Will surely be followed by a springtime of gladness.

The Soul, Like Nature, Has Seasons, Too

When you feel cast down and despondently sad
And you long to be happy and carefree and glad,
Do you ask yourself, as I so often do,
Why must there be days that are cheerless and blue?
Why is the song silenced in the heart that was gay?
And then I ask God what makes life this way,
And His explanation makes everything clear—
The soul has its seasons the same as the year.
Man, too, must pass through life's autumn of death
And have his heart frozen by winter's cold breath,
But spring always comes with new life and birth,
Followed by summer to warm the soft earth. . .
And oh, what a comfort to know there are reasons
That souls, like nature, must too
have their seasons—
Bounteous seasons and barren ones, too,
Times for rejoicing and times to be blue. . .
For with nothing but sameness
how dull life would be,
For only life's challenge can set the soul free. . .
And it takes a mixture of both bitter and sweet
To season our lives and make them complete.

Slowing Down

My days are so crowded and my hours so few
And I can no longer work fast like I used to do.
But I know I must learn to be satisfied,
That God has not completely denied
The joy of working—at a much slower pace—
For as long as He gives me a little place
To work with Him in His vineyard of love,
Just to know that He's helping me from above
Gives me strength to meet each day
As I travel along life's changing way.

APRIL

April comes with cheeks a-glowing,
Silver streams are all a-flowing,
Flowers open wide their eyes
In lovely rapturous surprise.
Lilies dream beside the brooks,
Violets in meadow nooks,
And the birds gone wild with glee
Fill the woods with melody.

Spring Awakens What Autumn Puts to Sleep

A garden of asters in varying hues,
Crimson pinks and violet blues,
Blossoming in the hazy fall,
Wrapped in autumn's lazy pall. . .
But early frost stole in one night,
And like a chilling, killing blight
It touched each pretty aster's head,
And now the garden's still and dead,
And all the lovely flowers that bloomed
Will soon be buried and entombed
In winter's icy shroud of snow. . .
But oh, how wonderful to know
That after winter comes the spring
To breathe new life in everything,
And all the flowers that fell in death
Will be awakened by spring's breath. . .
For in God's plan both men and flowers
Can only reach bright, shining hours
By dying first to rise in glory
And prove again the Easter story.

I Come to Meet You

I come to meet You, God, and as I linger here
I seem to feel You very near.
A rustling leaf, a rolling slope
Speak to my heart of endless hope.
The sun just rising in the sky,
The waking birdlings as they fly,
The grass all wet with morning dew
Are telling me I just met You. . .
And gently thus the day is born
As night gives way to breaking morn,
And once again I've met You, God,
And worshipped on Your holy sod. . .
For who could see the dawn break through
Without a glimpse of heaven and You?
For who but God could make the day
And softly put the night away?

All Nature Proclaims
Eternal Life

Flowers sleeping 'neath the snow,
Awakening when the spring winds blow,
Leafless trees so bare before
Gowned in lacy green once more,
Hard, unyielding, frozen sod
Now softly carpeted by God,
Still streams melting in the spring
Rippling over rocks that sing,
Barren, windswept, lonely hills
Turning gold with daffodils—
These miracles are all around
Within our sight and touch and sound,
As true and wonderful today
As when the stone was rolled away,
Proclaiming to all doubting men
That in God all things live again.

Growing Older Is Part of God's Plan

You can't hold back the dawn
or stop the tides from flowing
Or keep a rose from withering
or still a wind that's blowing,
And time cannot be halted in
its swift and endless flight,
For age is sure to follow youth
like day comes after night. . .
For He who sets our span of
years and watches from above
Replaces youth and beauty
with peace and truth and love,
And then our souls are privileged
to see a hidden treasure
That in youth escapes our eyes
in our pursuit of pleasure. . .
So passing years are but blessings
that open up the way
To the everlasting beauty
of God's eternal day.

Life's Golden Autumn

Memory opens wide the door
on a happy day like this,
And with a sweet nostalgia
we longingly recall,
The happy days of long ago
that seem the best of all. . .
But time cannot be halted in
its swift and endless flight,
And age is sure to follow youth
as day comes after night,
And once again it's proven that
the restless brain of man
Is powerless to alter God's great,
unchanging plan. . .
But while our steps grow slower
and we grow more tired, too,
The soul goes roaring upward
to realms untouched and new,
Where God's children live forever
in the beauty of His love.

Birthdays Are a Gift from God

Where does time go in its endless flight?
Spring turns to fall and day to night,
And birthdays come and birthdays go,
And where they go we do not know. . .
But God, who planned our life on earth
And gave our minds and bodies birth
And then enclosed a living soul
With heaven as the spirit's goal,
Has given man the gift of choice
To follow that small inner voice
That speaks to us from year to year,
Reminding us we've naught to fear. . .
For birthdays are a stepping stone
To endless joys as yet unknown —
So fill each day with happy things,
And may your burdens all take wing
And fly away and leave behind
Great joy of heart and peace of mind. . .
For birthdays are the gateway to
An endless life of joy for you
If you but pray from day to day
That He will show you the truth and the way.

Each Spring God Renews His Promise

⁕

Long, long ago in a land far away,
There came the dawn of the first Easter day,
And each year we see the promise reborn
That God gave the world on that first Easter morn.
For in each waking flower and each singing bird
The promise of Easter is witnessed and heard,
And spring is God's way of speaking to men
And renewing the promise of Easter again. . .
For death is a season that man must pass through,
And just like the flowers, God wakens him, too,
So why should we grieve when our loved ones die,
For we'll meet them again in a cloudless sky.
For Easter is more than a beautiful story —
It's the promise of life and eternal glory.

In God's Tomorrow
There Is Eternal Spring

All nature heeds the call of spring
as God awakens everything,
And all that seemed so dead and still
experiences a sudden thrill
As springtime lays a magic hand
across God's vast and fertile land.
Oh, the joy in standing by
to watch a sapphire springtime sky
Or see a fragile flower break through
what just a day ago or two
Seemed barren ground still hard with frost,
for in God's world, no life is lost,
And flowers sleep beneath the ground,
but when they hear spring's waking sound,
They push themselves through layers of clay
to reach the sunlight of God's day.
And man and woman, like flowers, too,
must sleep until called from the darkened deep
To live in that place where angels sing
and where there is eternal spring.

God's Unfailing Birthday Promise

From one birthday to another
God will gladly give
To everyone who seeks Him and
tries each day to live
A little bit more closely to
God and to each other,
Seeing everyone who passes as a
neighbor, friend, or brother,
Not only joy and happiness but
the faith to meet each trial
Not with fear and trepidation
but with an inner smile. . .
For we know life's never measured
by how many years we live
But by the kindly things we do
and the happiness we give.

TODAY'S JOY WAS BORN OF YESTERDAY'S SORROW

Who said the darkness of the
night would never turn to day?
Who said the winter's bleakness
would never pass away?
Who said the fog would never lift
and let the sunshine through?
Who said the skies, now overcast,
would nevermore be blue?
Why should we ever entertain
these thoughts so dark and grim
And let the brightness of our
minds grow cynical and dim
When we know beyond all
questioning that winter turns to spring
And on the notes of sorrow
new songs are made to sing?
For no one sheds a teardrop or suffers loss in vain,
Because God is always there to
turn our losses into gain. . .
And every burden borne today
and every present sorrow
Are but God's happy harbingers of a joyous,
bright tomorrow.

THE AUTUMN OF LIFE

What a wonderful time is life's autumn,
when the leaves of the trees are all gold,
When God fills each day as He sends
it with memories, priceless and old.
What a treasure-house filled with rare
jewels are the blessings of year upon year,
When life has been lived as you've lived it
in a home where God's presence is near. . .
May the deep meaning surrounding this day,
like the paintbrush of God up above,
Touch your life with wonderful blessings.

THIS IS JUST A RESTING PLACE

Sometimes the road of life seems
long as we travel through the years
And with a heart that's broken
and eyes brimful of tears,
We falter in our weariness
and sink beside the way,
But God leans down and whispers,
"Child, there'll be another day,"
And the road will grow much
smoother and much easier to face,
So do not be disheartened,
this is just a resting place.

THE POWER
OF PRAYER

The Heavenly Staircase

Prayers are the stairs that lead to God,
and there's joy every step of the way
When we make our pilgrimage to
Him with love in our hearts each day.

Power of Prayer

~~~

I am only a worker employed by the Lord,
And great is my gladness and rich my reward
If I can just spread the wonderful story
That God is the answer to eternal glory. . .
Bringing new hope and comfort and cheer
Telling sad hearts there is nothing to fear,
And what greater joy could there be than to share
The love of God and the power of prayer?

On the Wings of Prayer

On the wings of prayer our burdens take flight
And our load of care becomes bearably light
And our heavy hearts are lifted above
To be healed by the balm of God's wonderful love. . .
And the tears in our eyes are dried by the hands
Of a loving Father who understands
All of our problems, our fears and despair
When we take them to Him on the
wings of prayer.

The House of Prayer

Just close your eyes and open your heart
And feel your cares and worries depart.
Just yield yourself to the Father above
And let Him hold you secure in His love. . .
For life on earth grows more involved
With endless problems that can't be solved,
But God only asks us to do our best,
Then He will take over and finish the rest. . .
So when you are tired, discouraged, and blue,
There's always one door that is opened to you
And that is the door to the house of prayer,
And you'll find God waiting to meet you there. . .
And the house of prayer is no farther away
Than the quiet spot where you kneel and pray.
For the heart is a temple when God is there
As we place ourselves in His loving care. . .
And He hears every prayer and answers each one
When we pray in His name, "Thy will be done."
And the burdens that seemed too heavy to bear
Are lifted away on the wings of prayer.

God's Stairway

Step by step we climb day by day
Closer to God with each prayer we pray,
For the cry of the heart offered in prayer
Becomes just another spiritual stair
In the heavenly place where we live anew. . .
So never give up, for it's worth the climb
To live forever in endless time
Where the soul of man is safe and free
To live and love through eternity.

ANYWHERE IS A PLACE
OF PRAYER IF GOD IS THERE

I have prayed on my knees in the morning, I have
prayed as I walked along,
I have prayed in the silence and darkness, and
I've prayed to the tune of a song.
I have prayed in the midst of a triumph, and I've
prayed when I suffered defeat,
I have prayed on the sands of the seashore where
the waves of the ocean beat.
I have prayed in churches and chapels, cathedrals
and synagogues, too,
But often I had the feeling that my prayers were
not getting through. . .
And I realized then that our Father is not really
concerned when we pray
Or impressed by our manner of worship or the
eloquent words that we say.
He is only concerned with our feelings, and He
looks deep into our hearts
And hears the cry of our souls' deep need that no
words could ever impart. . .
So it isn't the prayer that's expressive or offered in
some special spot,
That's the sincere plea of a sinner, and God can
tell whether or not
We honestly seek His forgiveness and earnestly
mean what we say,
And then, and then only, God answers the prayers
that we fervently pray.

Begin Each Day by Kneeling to Pray

Start every day with a "good morning" prayer
And God will bless each thing you do
and keep you in His care. . .
And never, never sever the spirit's silken strand
That our Father up in heaven holds
in his mighty hand.

Show Me More Clearly the Way to Serve and Love You More Each Day

God, help me in my feeble way
To somehow do something each day
To show You that I love You best
And that my faith will stand each test,
And let me serve You every day
And feel You near me when I pray.
Oh, hear my prayer, dear God above,
And make me worthy of Your love.

Anxious Prayers

When we are deeply disturbed by a problem
and our minds are filled with doubt,
And we struggle to find a solution,
but there seems to be no way out,
We futilely keep on trying to
untangle our web of distress,
But our own little, puny efforts
meet with very little success.
And finally, exhausted and weary,
discouraged and downcast and low,
With no foreseeable answer and
with no other place to go,
We kneel down in sheer desperation
and slowly and stumblingly pray,
Then impatiently wait for an answer
in one sudden instant, we say,
"God does not seem to be listening,
so why should we bother to pray?"
But God can't get through to the anxious,
who are much too impatient to wait,
You must have faith to believe Him and
to know in your heart He'll be there.
So be not impatient or hasty,
just trust in the Lord and believe,
For whatever you ask in faith and love, in
abundance you are sure to receive.

$\mathcal{A}$ Part of Me

Dear God, You are a part of me —
You're all I do and all I see,
You're what I say and what I do,
For all my life belongs to You.
You walk with me and talk with me,
For I am Yours eternally,
And when I stumble, slip, and fall
Because I'm weak and lost and small,
You help me up and take my hand
And lead me toward the Promised Land.
I cannot dwell apart from You —
You would not ask or want me to,
For You have room within Your heart
To make each child of Yours a part
Of You and all Your love and care
If we but come to You in prayer.

Talk It Over with God

You're worried and troubled about everything,
Wondering and fearing what tomorrow will bring.
You long to tell someone, for you feel so alone,
But your friends are all burdened
with cares of their own.
There is only one place and only one friend
Who is never too busy, and you can always depend
On Him to be waiting, with arms open wide
To hear all the troubles you came to confide. . .
For the heavenly Father will always be there
When you seek Him and find Him at the
altar of prayer.

Listen in the Quietness

To try to run away from life is impossible to do,
For no matter where you chance to go,
your troubles will follow you;
For though the scenery is different,
when you look deep inside you'll find
The same deep, restless longings
that you thought you left behind.
So when life becomes a problem
much too great for us to bear,
Instead of trying to escape,
let us withdraw in prayer.
For withdrawal means renewal if
we withdraw to pray
And listen in the quietness to hear
what God will say.

Daily Prayers Are Heaven's Stairs

The stairway rises heaven-high,
the steps are dark and steep.
In weariness we climb them
as we stumble, fall, and weep.
And many times we falter
along the path of prayer,
Wondering if You hear us and
if You really care.
Oh, give us some assurance;
restore our faith anew,
So we can keep on climbing the
stairs of prayer to You.
For we are weak and wavering,
uncertain and unsure,
And only meeting You in prayer
can help us to endure
All life's trials and troubles, its sickness,
pain, and sorrow,
And give us strength and courage
to face and meet tomorrow.

PRAYERS CAN'T BE ANSWERED UNTIL THEY ARE PRAYED

Life without purpose is barren indeed,
There can't be a harvest unless you plant seed.
There can't be attainment unless there's a goal,
And man's but a robot unless there's a soul.
If we send no ships out, no ships will come in,
And unless there's a contest, nobody can win. . .
For games can't be won unless they are played,
And prayers can't be answered
unless they are prayed. . .
So whatever is wrong with your life today,
You'll find a solution if you kneel down and pray
Not just for pleasure, enjoyment, and health,
Not just for honors, prestige, and wealth,
But pray for a purpose to make life worth living,
And pray for the joy of unselfish giving. . .
For great is your gladness and rich your reward
When you make your life's purpose the
choice of the Lord.

ABIDING FAITH

Climb till Your Dream Comes True

Often your tasks will be many,
and more than you think you can do.
Often the road will be rugged,
and the hills insurmountable, too.
But always remember, the hills ahead
are never as steep as they seem,
And with faith in your heart, start upward
and climb till you reach your dream.
For nothing in life that is worthy
is ever too hard to achieve
If you have the courage to try it and
you have the faith to believe.
For faith is a force that is greater
than knowledge or power or skill,
And many defeats turn to triumphs
if you trust in God's wisdom and will.
For faith is a mover of mountains—
there's nothing that God cannot do—
So start out today with faith in your heart
and climb till your dream comes true.

ℱAITH AND TRUST

❧

Sometimes when a light
Goes out of our lives
And we are left in darkness
And we do not know which way to go,
We must put our hand
Into the hand of God
And ask Him to lead us
And if we let our lives become a prayer
Until we are strong enough
To stand under the weight
Of our own thoughts again,
Somehow, even the most difficult
Hours are bearable.

Help Us to See and Understand

God, give us wider vision to see and understand
That both the sunshine and the
showers are gifts from Thy great hand,
And when our lives are overcast
with trouble and with care,
Give us faith to see beyond
the dark clouds of despair,
And teach us that it takes the showers
to make the flowers grow,
And only in the storms of life when
the winds of trouble blow
Can man, too, reach maturity and
grow in faith and grace
And gain the strength and courage
to enable him to face
Sunny days as well as rain,
high peaks as well as low,
Knowing that the April showers
will make May flowers grow. . .
And then at last may we accept
the sunshine and the shower,
Confident it takes them both to make salvation ours.

The Bend in the Road

Sometimes we come to life's crossroads
and view what we think is the end,
But God has a much wider vision,
and He knows it's only a bend.
The road will go on and get smoother,
and after we've stopped for a rest,
The path that lies hidden beyond
us is often the part that is best.
So rest and relax and grow stronger,
let go and let God share your load,
And have faith in a brighter tomorrow;
you've just come to a bend in the road.

Trust God

Take heart and meet each minute
with faith in God's great love,
Aware that every day of life is
controlled by God above. . .
And never dread tomorrow
or what the future brings —
Just pray for strength and courage
and trust God in all things.

Now I Lay Me Down to Sleep

I remember so well this prayer I said
Each night as my mother tucked me in bed,
And today this same prayer is still the best way
To sign off with God at the end of the day
And to ask Him your soul to safely keep
As you wearily close your tired eyes in sleep,
Feeling content that the Father above
Will hold you secure in His great arms of love. . .
And having His promise that if ere you wake
His angels reach down, your sweet soul to take
Is perfect assurance that, awake or asleep,
God is always right there to tenderly keep
All of His children ever safe in His care,
For God's here and He's there
and He's everywhere. . .
So into His hands each night as I sleep
I commend my soul for the dear Lord to keep,
Knowing that if my soul should take flight
It will soar to the land where there is no night.

Finding Faith in a Flower

Sometimes when faith is running low
And I cannot fathom why things are so,
I walk among the flowers that grow
And learn the answers to all I would know. . .
For among my flowers I have come to see
Life's miracle and its mystery,
And standing in silence and reverie,
My faith comes flooding back to me.

Yesterday, Today, and Tomorrow

Yesterday's dead, tomorrow's unborn,
So there's nothing to fear and nothing to mourn,
For all that is past and all that has been
Can never return to be lived once again. . .
And what lies ahead or the things that will be
Are still in God's hands, so it is not up to me
To live in the future that is God's great unknown,
For the past and the present
God claims for His own. . .
So all I need do is to live for today
And trust God to show me the truth and the way,
For it's only the memory of things that have been
And expecting tomorrow to bring trouble again
That fills my today, which God wants to bless,
With uncertain fears and borrowed distress. . .
For all I need live for is this one little minute,
For life's here and now and eternity's in it.

THE HEAVENS DECLARE
THE GLORY OF GOD

You ask me how I know it's
true that there is a living God.
A God who rules the universe—
the sky, the sea, the sod—
A God who holds all creatures
in the hollow of His hand,
A God who put infinity in one tiny grain of sand,
A God who made the seasons—
winter, summer, fall, and spring—
And put His flawless rhythm
into each created thing,
A God who hangs the sun out
slowly with the break of day
And gently takes the stars in
and puts the night away,
A God whose mighty handiwork
defies the skill of man,
For no architect can alter
God's perfect master plan.
What better answers are there
to prove His holy being
Than the wonders all around us
that are ours just for the seeing.

Somebody Loves You

~~~~~

Somebody loves you more than you know,
Somebody goes with you wherever you go,
Somebody really and truly cares
And lovingly listens to all of your prayers. . .
Don't doubt for a minute that this is not true,
For God loves His children and
takes care of them, too. . .
And all of His treasures are yours to share
If you love Him completely and
show that you care. . .
And if you walk in His footsteps
and have faith to believe,
There's nothing you ask for that
you will not receive!

The Revelations of Easter

The waking earth in springtime
Reminds us it is true
That nothing ever really dies
That is not born anew. . .
So trust God's all-wise wisdom
And doubt the Father never,
For in His heavenly kingdom
There is nothing lost forever.

Fortress of Faith

It's easy to say "In God we trust"
when life is radiant and fair,
But the test of faith is only found
when there are burdens to bear.
For our claim to faith in the
sunshine is really no faith at all,
For when roads are smooth and days
are bright our need for God is so small.
And no one discovers the fullness
or the greatness of God's love
Unless they have walked in the
darkness with only a light from above.
For the faith to endure whatever comes
is born of sorrow and trials
And strengthened only by discipline
and nurtured by self-denials.
So be not disheartened by troubles,
for trials are the building blocks
On which to erect a fortress of faith,
secure on God's ageless rocks.

Faith Is a Candle

In this sick world of hatred and violence and sin,
Where society renounces morals
and rejects discipline,
We stumble in darkness groping vainly for light
To distinguish the difference between
wrong and right.
But dawn cannot follow this night of despair
Unless faith lights a candle in
all hearts everywhere.
And warmed by the glow, our hate melts away
And love lights the path to a peaceful new day.

He Asks so Little and Gives so Much

⁂

What must I do to ensure peace of mind?
Is the answer I'm seeking too hard to find?
How can I know what God wants me to be?
How can I tell what's expected of me?
Where can I go for guidance and aid
To help me correct the errors I've made?
The answer is found in doing three things,
And great is the gladness that doing them brings.
"Do justice"—"Love kindness"—
"Walk humbly with God"—
For with these three things as
your rule and your rod,
All things worth having are yours to achieve,
If you follow God's words and have
faith to believe.

We Can't, but God Can

Why things happen as they do
we do not always know,
And we cannot always fathom
why our spirits sink so low.
But all that is required of us
whenever things go wrong
Is to trust in God implicitly with
a faith that's deep and strong.
And while He may not instantly
unravel all the strands
Of the tangled thoughts that trouble us,
He completely understands—
And in His time, if we have faith,
He will gradually restore
The brightness to our spirits
that we've been longing for.
So remember there's no cloud too
dark for God's light to penetrate
If we keep on believing and have
faith enough to wait.

FAITH IS A MOVER OF MOUNTAINS

Faith is a force that is greater
than knowledge or power or skill,
And the darkest defeat turns to triumph
if you trust in God's wisdom and will,
For faith is a mover of mountains—
there's nothing man cannot achieve
If he has the courage to try it
and then has the faith to believe.

ETERNAL BLESSINGS

$\mathcal{G}$OD'S JEWELS FOR YOU

We watch the rich and famous
bedecked in precious jewels,
Enjoying earthly pleasures, defying moral rules,
And in our mood of discontent
we sink into despair
And long for earthly riches and
feel cheated of our share. . .
But stop these idle musings,
God has stored up for you
Treasures that are far beyond
earth's jewels and riches, too,
For never, never discount
what God has promised man
If he will walk in meekness
and accept God's flawless plan,
For if we heed His teaching as
we journey through the years,
We'll find the richest jewels of
all are crystallized from tears.

THERE ARE BLESSINGS IN EVERYTHING

Blessings come in many guises
That God alone in love devises,
And sickness, which we dread so much,
Can bring a very healing touch,
For often on the wings of pain
The peace we sought before in vain
Will come to us with sweet surprise,
For God is merciful and wise. . .
And through long hours of tribulation
God gives us time for meditation,
And no sickness can be counted loss
That teaches us to bear our cross.

THE BLESSINGS OF SHARING

Only what we give away
Enriches us from day to day,
For not in getting but in giving
Is found the lasting joy of living,
For no one ever had a part
In sharing treasures of the heart
Who did not feel the impact of
The magic mystery of God's love.
Love alone can make us kind
And give us joy and peace of mind,
So live with joy unselfishly,
And you'll be blessed abundantly.

BLESSING IN DISGUISE

God sends His little angels
in many forms and guises.
They come as lovely miracles
that God alone devises,
For every little angel with a body bent or broken
Or a little mind challenged
or little words unspoken
Is just God's way of trying to reach
out and touch the hands
Of all who do not know Him
and cannot understand
That often through an angel
whose wings will never fly
The Lord is pointing out the
way to His eternal sky,
Where there will be no handicaps
of body, soul, or mind,
And where all limitations will
be dropped and left behind. . .
So accept these little angels
as gifts from God above,
And thank Him for this lesson
in faith and hope and love.

What Is a Baby?

A baby is a gift of life born
of the wonder of love—
A little bit of eternity sent from the Father above,
Giving a new dimension to the love
between husband and wife
And putting an added new meaning
to the wonder and mystery of life.

MOTHERHOOD

The dearest gifts that heaven holds,
the very finest, too,
Were made into one pattern that
was perfect, sweet, and true.
The angels smiled, well pleased, and said,
"Compared to all the others,
This pattern is so wonderful let's
use it just for mothers!"
And through the years, a mother has
been all that's sweet and good,
For there's a bit of God and love
in all true motherhood.

THE GOLDEN YEARS OF LIFE

God in His loving and all-wise way
Makes the heart that once was too young yesterday
Serene and more gentle and less restless, too,
Content to remember the joys it once knew.
And all that we sought on the pathway of pleasure
Becomes but a memory to cherish and treasure —
The fast pace grows slower and the spirit serene,
And the soul can envision what
the eyes have not seen.
And so while life's springtime is sweet to recall,
The autumn of life is the best time of all,
For our wild youthful yearnings all gradually cease,
And God fills our days with beauty and peace!

A TIME OF RENEWAL AND SPIRITUAL BLESSING

No one likes to be sick, and yet we know
It takes sunshine and rain to make flowers grow,
And if we never were sick and we never felt pain,
We'd be like a desert without any rain.
And who wants a life that is barren and dry
With never a cloud to darken the sky?
For continuous sun goes unrecognized
Like the blessings God sends,
which are often disguised,
For sometimes a sickness that seems so distressing
Is a time of renewal and spiritual blessing.

Beyond Our Asking

More than hearts can imagine
or minds comprehend,
God's bountiful gifts are ours without end.
We ask for a cupful when the vast sea is ours,
We pick a small rosebud from a garden of flowers,
We reach for a sunbeam but the sun still abides,
We draw one short breath but there's air on all sides.
Whatever we ask for falls short of God's giving,
For His greatness exceeds every facet of living
And always God's ready and eager and willing
To pour out His mercy, completely fulfilling
All of man's needs for peace, joy, and rest,
For God gives His children whatever is best.
Just give Him a chance to open His treasures,
And He'll fill your life with
unfathomable pleasures—
Pleasures that never grow worn out and faded
And leave us depleted disillusioned and jaded—
For God has a storehouse just filled to the brim
With all that man needs, if we'll only ask Him.

Not by Chance of Happenstance

Into our lives come many things
to break the dull routine—
The things we had not planned
on that happen unforeseen,
The unexpected little joys that
are scattered on our way,
Success we did not count on
or a rare, fulfilling day,
A catchy, lilting melody that
makes us want to dance,
A nameless exaltation of
enchantment and romance,
The sudden, unplanned meeting
that comes with sweet surprise
And lights the heart with happiness
like a rainbow in the skies.
Now some folks call it fickle fate
and some folks call it chance
While others just accept it
as a pleasant happenstance,
But no matter what you call it,
it didn't come without design,
For all our lives are fashioned
by the hand that is divine.

MEMORIES

Tender little memories
Of some word or deed
Give us strength and courage
When we are in need.
Blessed little memories
Help us bear the cross
And soften all the bitterness
Of failure and loss.
Precious little memories
Of little things we've done
Make the very darkest day
A bright and happy one.

Heart Gifts

It's not the things that can be bought
That are life's richest treasures,
It's just the little gifts from the heart
That money cannot measure.
A cheerful smile, a friendly word,
A sympathetic nod,
All priceless little treasures
From the storehouse of our God.
They are the things that can't be bought
With silver or with gold,
For thoughtfulness and kindness
And love are never sold.
They are the priceless things in life
For which no one can pay,
And the giver finds rich recompense
In giving them away.

THIS IS MY FATHER'S WORLD

Everywhere across the land
You see God's face and touch His hand
Each time you look up in the sky
Or watch the fluffy clouds drift by,
Or feel the sunshine, warm and bright,
Or watch the dark night turn to light,
Or hear a bluebird brightly sing,
Or see the winter turn to spring,
Or stop to pick a daffodil,
Or gather violets on some hill,
Or touch a leaf or see a tree,
It's all God whispering, "This is Me.
And I am faith and I am light,
And in Me there shall be no night."

God's Keeping

❧

To be in God's keeping is surely a blessing,
For though life is often dark and distressing,
No day is too dark and no burden too great
That God in His love cannot penetrate.

TRIUMPH OVER TRIALS

Traveling to Heaven

Life is a highway on which the years go by,
Sometimes the road is level,
sometimes the hills are high.
But as we travel onward to
a future that's unknown,
We can make each mile we travel
a heavenly stepping stone!

Wish Not for Ease
or to Do as You Please

If wishes worked like magic
and plans worked that way, too,
And if everything you wished for,
whether good or bad for you,
Immediately were granted with
no effort on your part,
You'd experience no fulfillment
of your spirit or your heart.
For things achieved too easily
lose their charm and meaning, too,
For it is life's difficulties and
the trial times we go through
That make us strong in spirit
and endow us with the will
To surmount the insurmountable
and to climb the highest hill.
So wish not for the easy way
to win your heart's desire,
For the joy's in overcoming
and withstanding flood and fire,
For to triumph over trouble
and grow stronger with defeat
Is to win the kind of victory
that will make your life complete.

Let Daily Prayers Dissolve Your Cares

We all have cares and problems
we cannot solve alone,
But if we go to God in prayer,
we are never on our own,
And no day is unmeetable if
on rising, our first thought
Is to thank God for the blessings
that His loving care has brought,
For there can be no failures
or hopeless, unsaved sinners
If we enlist the help of God,
who makes all losers winners. . .
So meet Him in the morning
and go with Him through the day
And thank Him for His guidance
each evening when you pray,
And if you follow faithfully this daily way to pray,
You will never in your lifetime
face another hopeless day. . .
For like a soaring eagle, you, too, can rise above
The storms of life around you on
the wings of prayer and love.

Be of Good Cheer, There's Nothing to Fear

Cheerful thoughts like sunbeams
lighten up the darkest fears,
For when the heart is happy
there's just no time for tears,
And when the face is smiling
it's impossible to frown,
And when you are high-spirited
you cannot feel low-down. . .
For the nature of our attitudes
toward circumstantial things
Determines our acceptance of
the problems that life brings,
And since fear and dread and
worry cannot help in any way,
It's much healthier and happier
to be cheerful every day. . .
And if you'll only try it, you will find,
without a doubt,
A cheerful attitude's something
no one should be without,
For when the heart is cheerful,
it cannot be filled with fear,
And without fear, the way ahead
seems more distinct and clear,
And we realize there's nothing
that we must face alone,
For our heavenly Father loves us,
and our problems are His own.

Burdens Can Be Blessings

Our Father knows what's best for us,
So why should we complain—
We always want the sunshine,
But He knows there must be rain—
We love the sound of laughter
And the merriment of cheer,
But our hearts would lose their tenderness
If we never shed a tear. . .
So whenever we are troubled
And life has lost its song
It's God testing us with burdens
Just to make our spirit strong!

BRIGHTEN THE CORNER
WHERE YOU ARE

We cannot all be famous or be
listed in "Who's Who,"
But every person, great or small,
has important work to do. . .
For seldom do we realize the
importance of small deeds
Or to what degree of greatness
unnoticed kindness leads. . .
So do not sit and idly wish
for wider, new dimensions
Where you can put in practice
your many good intentions,
But at the spot God placed you,
begin at once to do
Little things to brighten up
the lives surrounding you. . .
For if everybody brightened up the
spot on which they're standing
By being more considerate and
a little less demanding,
This dark old world would very
soon eclipse the evening star
If everybody brightened up the
corner where they are.

THE HOME BEYOND

We feel so sad when those we love
Are called to live in the home above,
But why should we grieve when they say good-bye
And go to dwell in a cloudless sky?
For they have but gone to prepare the way,
And we'll meet them again some happy day,
For God has told us that nothing can sever
A life He created to live forever.
So let God's promise soften our sorrow
And give us new strength for a brighter tomorrow.

My Birthday in Bethesda

How little we know what God has in store
As daily He blesses our lives more and more.
I've lived many years and I've learned many things,
But today I have grown new spiritual wings. . .
For pain has a way of broadening our view
And bringing us closer in sympathy, too,
To those who are living in constant pain
And trying somehow to bravely sustain
The faith and endurance to keep on trying
When they almost welcome the peace of dying. . .
Without this experience I would have lived and died
Without fathoming the pain of Christ crucified,
For none of us knows what pain is all about
Until our spiritual wings start to sprout.
So thank You, God, for the gift You sent
To teach me that pain's heaven-sent.

Life's Disappointments Are God's Sweetest Appointments

Out of life's misery born of man's sins,
A fuller, richer life begins,
For when we are helpless with no place to go
And our hearts are heavy and our spirits are low,
If we place our lives in God's hands
And surrender completely to His will and demands,
The darkness lifts and the sun shines through,
And by His touch we are born anew.
So praise God for trouble that cuts like a knife
And disappointments that shatter your life,
For with patience to wait and faith to endure,
Your life will be blessed and your future secure,
For God is but testing your faith and your love
Before He appoints you to rise far above
All the small things that so sorely distress you,
For God's only intention is to
strengthen and bless you.

FAITH FOR DARK DAYS

When dark days come—and they come to us all—
We feel so helpless and lost and small.
We cannot fathom the reason why,
And it is futile for us to try
To find the answer, the reason or cause,
For the master plan is without any flaws.
And when the darkness shuts out the light,
We must lean on faith to restore our sight,
For there is nothing we need know
If we have faith that wherever we go
God will be there to help us to bear
Our disappointments, pain, and care.
For He is our shepherd, our Father, our Guide,
And you're never alone with the Lord at your side.
So may the great Physician attend you,
And may His healing completely mend you.

Worry No More—
God Knows the Score

Have you ever been caught in
a web you didn't weave,
Involved in conditions that are hard to believe?
Have you ever felt you must speak
and explain and deny
A story that's groundless or a small, whispered lie?
Have you ever heard rumors
you would like to refute
Or some telltale gossip you would like to dispute?
Well, don't be upset, for God knows the score,
And with God as your judge you
need worry no more.
For men may misjudge you, but God's verdict is fair,
For He looks deep inside and is deeply aware
Of every small detail in your pattern of living,
And always He's fair and lenient and forgiving,
And knowing that God is your
judge and your jury
Frees you completely from
man's falseness and fury.
And secure in this knowledge,
let your thoughts rise above
Man's small, shallow judgments
that are so empty of
God's goodness and greatness in judging men,
And forget ugly rumors and be happy again.

My Daily Prayer

God, be my resting place and my protection
In hours of trouble, defeat, and dejection.
May I never give way to self-pity and sorrow,
May I always be sure of a better tomorrow,
May I stand undaunted come what may,
Secure in the knowledge I have only to pray
And ask my Creator and Father above
To keep me serene in His grace and His love.

INDEX